Construction Trucks

Julie Murray

Abdo Kids Junior
is an Imprint of Abdo Kids
abdobooks.com

Abdo
TRUCKS AT WORK
Kids

abdobooks.com

Published by Abdo Kids, a division of ABDO, P.O. Box 398166, Minneapolis, Minnesota 55439. Copyright © 2024 by Abdo Consulting Group, Inc. International copyrights reserved in all countries. No part of this book may be reproduced in any form without written permission from the publisher. Abdo Kids Junior™ is a trademark and logo of Abdo Kids.

Printed in the United States of America, North Mankato, Minnesota.
052023
092023

Photo Credits: Getty Images, Shutterstock, ©Ditch Witch p.22/ CC BY 2.0

Production Contributors: Teddy Borth, Jennie Forsberg, Grace Hansen

Design Contributors: Candice Keimig, Pakou Moua

Library of Congress Control Number: 2022946716

Publisher's Cataloging-in-Publication Data

Names: Murray, Julie, author.

Title: Construction trucks / by Julie Murray

Description: Minneapolis, Minnesota : Abdo Kids, 2024 | Series: Trucks at work | Includes online resources and index.

Identifiers: ISBN 9781098266127 (lib. bdg.) | ISBN 9781098266820 (ebook) | ISBN 9781098267179 (Read-to-me ebook)

Subjects: LCSH: Trucks--Juvenile literature. | Vehicles--Juvenile literature. | Construction equipment--Juvenile literature.

Classification: DDC 388.32--dc23

Table of Contents

Construction Trucks . .4

More Construction Trucks 22

Glossary 23

Index 24

Abdo Kids Code 24

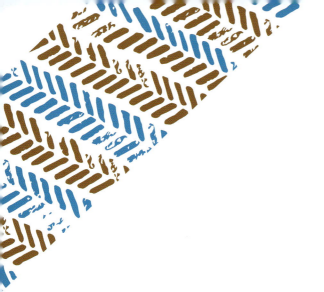

Construction Trucks

There are lots of construction trucks!

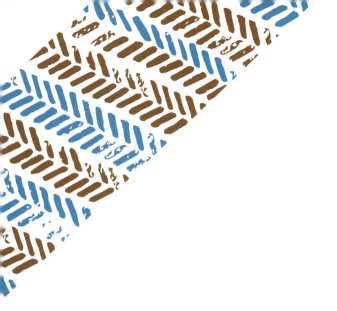

The dump truck carries a big dirt load.

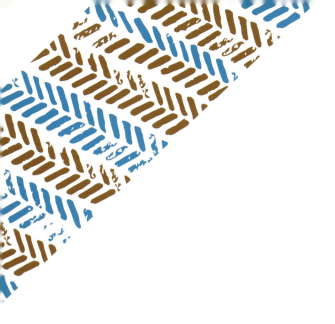

Liz drives the backhoe.

She digs a hole.

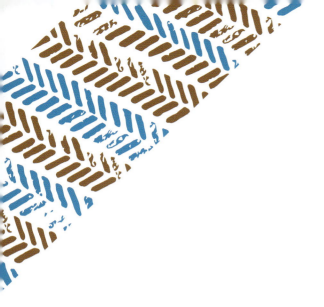

A boom truck has a **crane**.

It lifts heavy items.

A bulldozer helps move dirt and rocks.

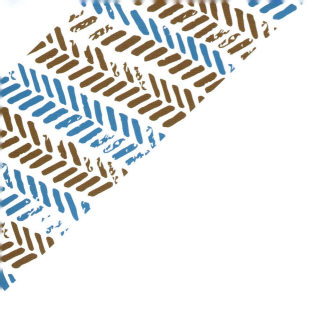

A concrete mixer has a drum that spins. Concrete moves down the **chute**.

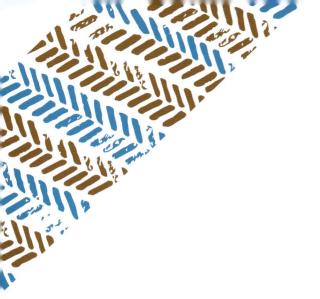

Gus drives a front loader.

He dumps the dirt.

A grader makes the dirt even.

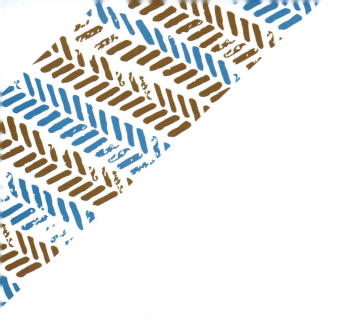

Have you seen any of these trucks?

More Construction Trucks

compactor

excavator

forklift

trencher

Glossary

chute
a passage down which things can slide.

crane
a machine with a tall arm that can move up and down or in a circle to lift and move heavy objects.

Index

backhoe 8

boom truck 10

bulldozer 12

concrete mixer 14

dump truck 6

front loader 16

grader 18

Visit **abdokids.com** to access crafts, games, videos, and more!

Use Abdo Kids code **TCK6127** or scan this QR code!